THE
WITCH
WITHIN

Dedicated to all
those who are
seeking the path,
the way of the witch,
the kiss of magic.

THE
WITCH
WITHIN

Discover The
Type of Witch You Are

TUDORBETH

Hardie Grant

BOOKS

CONTENTS

WELCOME ✳ WONDERFUL WITCHES

What does it mean to be a witch in the 21st century?

There is a bit more to witchcraft than black cats, pointy hats and broomsticks. Sure, these are used by the many different types of witches you will find in this book, but generally these are symbols of a past that has influenced the present. Witchcraft has changed from the time in which we cooked on cauldrons and swept the floors with a good broom. There is now a veritable rainbow of witch types, all with their own unique practices and focuses.

This book is for those who are seeking the path of the witch, and it is intended to help you find your way through all the different types of witches. You may resonate with one type or have something in common with all of them (in which case, you are probably an Eclectic Witch). Each one of the witch types will be explored, and a description of the type of practice will also highlight the ways of that specific witch.

This book has been designed to be interactive. You could read it on your own or in a group of like-minded friends for a witchy evening. Each section of witches is preceded by a set of ten questions, for which you can choose A, B, C, D or E answers. These answers help you to decide what type of witch you may be - but remember, you may have many answers that resonate with you, as we are all made of different characteristics. No two witches - and, for that matter, no two people - are identical. We may be similar,

but we are all unique. Furthermore, as we grow and develop, our witchcraft type and practice can also change. I was born as a Hereditary Witch, and for many years I thought I was a White Witch, but as the years progressed and I have found my own path, I realise now I am more of a Hedgewitch than anything.

When you read the answers, you may get a tingly sensation or a sudden feeling: this is your instinctive response, and it is showing you which answer is the right one. Follow your feelings and especially your first thoughts, as these stem straight from your soul and are an unconscious decision. If you linger and dissect each answer, you are adding conscious awareness. Witchcraft is about following instinct and therefore our true selves. Learning to follow your initial instincts is the first step on a witch's path.

The witch types are categorised into five different groups: Colour Witches, Nature Witches, Mystical Witches, Traditional Witches and Creative Witches. Each of these groups has a specific theme running through it. For example, all the witch types within the nature group follow a generic nature theme, but there are subtle differences within each type that distinguish their magical practice. You may resonate with one distinctive type in this group, or all. In addition, you may find yourself resonating with all the groups, which is equally acceptable. Always remember that witchcraft stems from you, and what follows in this book are examples of the many wondrous types there are to choose from.

For each of the specific witch types, I will share the characteristics, lucky colour, lucky animal, magical practices and strengths, as well as the signs that show you could be that type of witch. For each witch type, there is also a form of magical practice for you to try, such as a spell, potion or charm. A word of warning when performing magic, though: always keep love and light in your heart.

There are specific rules within witchcraft, and one of them is that we never wish or cast for someone against their will. Free will is a powerful gift we have been given and it is something that requires the deepest respect. For example, you may desire someone, but they may not feel the same way about you. Magic should always be used for good, for healing and for receiving that which we desire without bending the will of another or of any living presence.

If you wish to 'hex', or want to bend someone's will to your own, then this is not the book for you! Hexing is not what witchcraft is about. We do not cast ill will on to anyone, as there will be repercussions. All that we wish for will return to us three-fold! In other words, what we put out, we will receive back, at three times the power. It's a bit like the old saying 'You reap what you sow.' Therefore, be mindful of what you say and how you use magic.

And now we turn to the witch types themselves and the specific groups.

I hope you enjoy this book – and welcome to the wonderful world of witches.

Blessed be,
Tudorbeth

WITCH TYPES AT A GLANCE

WITCH TYPE	CHARACTER	LUCKY COLOUR
Grey	Strong, independent	Grey
Red	Loving, affectionate	Red
Green	Honest, communicative	Green
White	Compassionate, empathetic	White
Blue	Healing, wise	Blue
Weather	Intense, powerful	Silver
Sea	Changeable, secretive	Turquoise
Traditional	Conventional, conformist	Brown
Elemental	Grounded, decisive	Olive
Jewel	Scientific, analytical	Gold
Lunar	Mysterious, beguiling	Lilac
Cosmic	Energetic, expansive	Indigo
Zodiac	Inquisitive, truthful	Maroon
Divination	Psychic, knowledgeable	Yellow
Fae	Innocent, gentle	Fuchsia
Hedgewitch	Imaginative, free	Pink
Hereditary	Aloof, biased	Cyan
Eclectic	Changeable, flexible	Cream
Intuitive	Instinctive, trusting	Purple
Wiccan	Team-player, dependable	Black
Kitchen	Organised, experimental	Teal
Art	Dreamy, quirky	Magenta
Book	Studious, solitary	Navy blue
Hexafoil	Captivating, methodical	Orange
Practical	Resourceful, frugal	Burgundy

LUCKY ANIMAL	MAGICAL PRACTICE	MAGICAL SPECIALITY
Moth	Shadow	Protection spells
Salamander	Love	Love charms
Horse	Earth	Flower spells
Caterpillar	Spiritual guidance	Visualisation magic
Dolphin	Meditation	Healing tonics
Robin	Weather	Storm spells
Frog	Water	Potions and brews
Ant	Correspondence	Traditional spells
Bumble bee	Elemental	Seasonal spells
Dragonfly	Crystal	Crystal elixirs
Owl	Moon	Lunar correspondence spells
Spider	Cosmic energy	Eclipse spells
Hare	Astrological	Planetary spells
Butterfly	Divination	Scrying spells
Mouse	Fairy	Fairy spells
Rabbit	Nature	Travelling spells
Cat	Ancestral	Spells and charms
Goose	Anything they choose	Spells and potions
Dog	Energy	Empathy spells
Crow	Traditional	Ritual spells
Sheep	Manifestation	Brews and potions
Swallow	Visual	Colour spells
Tortoise	Grimoire	Knowledge spells
Duck	Pattern	Sigil spells
Fox	Practical	Charms, brews

THE GENERAL QUIZ

The chapters of this book are designed around different groups: Colour Witches, Nature Witches, Mystical Witches, Traditional Witches and Creative Witches. Within each group, there are different types of witch, from the Sea Witch to the Book Witch. Before you begin to delve into your specific witch type, perhaps you would like to complete this general quiz to see which overall group you might belong to before looking more deeply into your specific type.

Remember, though: it is perfectly alright to resonate with one or more groups. We are all made up of different interests, preferences and likes and dislikes. This quiz will just help to steer you in the direction that suits you best.

Which aesthetic do you prefer?

a. fairycore
b. grandmacore
c. naturecore
d. witchcore
e. animalcore

What is your ideal pastime?

a. delving into esoteric arts, such as tarot, Ouija or astrology
b. reading anything and everything
c. walking
d. cooking
e. gardening

You prefer to be:

a. visiting old buildings and historic places
b. in the kitchen
c. at the beach
d. in the park
e. helping out at an animal sanctuary

You are interested in:

a. the universe/cosmos
b. art and crafts
c. the weather
d. the Earth
e. feelings and emotions

Which of these makes you experience physical sensations?

a. anything supernatural, such as ghost hunting
b. viewing a particular piece of art
c. a good thunderstorm
d. a romantic/sad film
e. colours, e.g. blue makes you physically feel cold, etc.

Your favourite drink is:

a. anything
b. coffee
c. herbal tea
d. traditional tea or water
e. red/white wine, including prosecco

Your favourite season is:

a. winter
b. spring
c. summer
d. autumn
e. all of them

When you go for a walk in nature, you always:

a. look for fairies/magical creatures/ghosts
b. look at the patterns and shapes of leaves and flora
c. look at the cloud formations
d. collect pine cones, stones, tree bark, etc.
e. notice the colour of the trees and plants first

MOSTLY AS: MYSTICAL WITCH

If you have scored mostly As, then begin with the chapter on Mystical Witches (pages 66-89). Here, you will find five distinct types of witches: the Lunar Witch, the Cosmic Witch, the Zodiac Witch, the Divination Witch and finally the Fae Witch. As each of their names imply, Mystical Witches seek out mysterious realms and esoteric beliefs, such as the many different forms of divination or astrology.

MOSTLY BS: CREATIVE WITCH

If you have answered mostly Bs, then you are in the realm of the Creative Witches (pages 114-137), whose enterprising and innovative ways coincide with their magical practice. In this chapter, you will learn about the different Creative Witch types, including the mouthwatering delights of the Kitchen Witch, the beauty-loving Art Witch, the studious Book Witch, the symbol-focused Hexafoil Witch and finally the Practical Witch.

MOSTLY CS: NATURE WITCH

If you have answered mostly Cs, then you can begin your journey into witch types with the chapter on Nature Witches (pages 42-65). Here you will find the Sea Witch, along with the Weather Witch, the Traditional Witch, the Elemental Witch and finally the Jewel Witch.

MOSTLY DS: TRADITIONAL WITCH

If you have scored mostly Ds, then the chapter on Traditional Witches (pages 90-113) is a good starting point for you. Traditional Witches embody the most common or well-known witch types: the Wiccan Witch, the Eclectic Witch, the Hedgewitch, the Hereditary Witch and the Intuitive Witch.

MOSTLY ES: COLOUR WITCH

If you have scored mostly Es, then you can begin your witch-type journey with the first chapter, which is all about Colour Witches (pages 18-41). These have grown in popularity in recent years, and we now have the Red Witch, the Green Witch and the White Witch, along with the Grey Witch and the newly arrived Blue Witch, who cares deeply about the planet and the animal kingdom.

WITCH TYPES

COLOUR WITCHES

In this group of witches, we shall explore the many wondrous colour types. These have grown in recent years, and we no longer have just the White Witch, who so captivated us in stories and fairy tales. There are now Green Witches, Red Witches, Grey Witches and Blue Witches, and all have a specific focus on a distinct branch of magic. For example, Red Witches will concern themselves with all aspects of love, including friendships, marriage and even the love of pets, while a Grey Witch will specialise in magical practices that are protective and defensive. All these colour witches have a unique emphasis to their magic. Answer these questions to see if you are one of them – or you may resonate with all of them, in which case you most certainly are a Rainbow Witch (a mix of all the colours).

Your favourite colours are:

a. blacks, whites, greys
b. reds, pinks, pastels
c. greens, browns, yellows
d. purples, metallics, gold/silver
e. blues, indigos, aquamarine

Your favourite season is:

a. winter
b. spring
c. summer
d. autumn
e. all year

Your favourite scents are:

a. clean tones, like fresh linen, sea breeze
b. sweet tones, like magnolia, vanilla
c. woody tones, like oakmoss, pine
d. fruity tones, like peaches, citrus
e. musky tones, like leather, myrrh

Your favourite foods are:

a. meats/fish
b. sweet foods
c. herb flavours
d. vegetables/fruits
e. savoury dishes

Your favourite subjects at school were:

a. science
b. literature
c. you hated school with a passion
d. home economics
e. maths

Your ideal job/career is:

a. military service
b. entertainment (singer/dancer/actor)
c. chef/serving the public
d. educational
e. nurse/doctor/care work

Your ideal night out with friends would be:

a. local pub
b. meal in a posh restaurant
c. staying in and ordering a takeaway (takeout)
d. cinema/theatre
e. nightclub/disco

Your favourite clothes are:

a. dramatic statement pieces
b. romantic styles
c. bohemian styles
d. casual jeans and T-shirts
e. anything you can find

Your ideal method of transport is:

a. public transport
b. sports car/convertible
c. walking
d. aeroplane/boat
e. cycle

Your favourite animal is:

a. cat
b. rabbit
c. horse
d. fish
e. dog

MOSTLY AS: GREY WITCH

The Grey Witch is a practitioner of both black and white magic. They have been known to seek revenge in certain ways on those who may have wronged them but generally their magic is used defensively. Grey Witches have great protection spells to shield them from negative forces.

MOSTLY BS: RED WITCH

The Red Witch is a witch who specifically deals with love, sex and romance. They are the witch who knows everything there is about love in all its many forms. They are also a powerful purveyor of love potions and charms, and can may exude a powerful aura of sexuality. This witch's magic is all about love, marriage, sex, relationships, divorce, break-ups, make-ups and mash-ups.

MOSTLY CS: GREEN WITCH

A Green Witch is very much an Earth Witch, in the sense that they work with the earth. Flora and fauna feature front and centre in their magical practice, and they are also avid foragers. These are the witches whose gardens are simply awe-inspiring, and they work closely with energies of the earth such as nymphs and forest sprites.

MOSTLY DS: WHITE WITCH

This witch is not to be confused with the White Witch from *The Chronicles of Narnia*. Our White Witch is not a frosty ice queen; indeed, they are full of love and warmth, and work for light and goodness. The White Witch is a witch who works first and foremost for the greater good and is loyal and true to all their loved ones, as well as strangers who need their help.

MOSTLY ES: BLUE WITCH

The Blue Witch is solely concerned with all aspects of healing. They are often regarded as being rather clinical and matter-of-fact, and very focused on their healthy pursuits. These witches can also be misunderstood and labelled as selfish, because they know that in order to heal others, one must begin with oneself.

THE GREY WITCH

CHARACTER
Strong, independent,
balanced, outspoken

LUCKY COLOUR
Grey

LUCKY ANIMAL
Moth

MAGICAL PRACTICE
Shadow magic in all its many
forms, both light and dark,
protection magic, defensive magic

DESCRIPTION

The Grey Witch is not averse to practising shadow magic: that is, magic that some would consider dark magic or the black arts. This is because the Grey Witch knows that we live in a world of duality. There is black and white, there is light and dark, there is good and bad, and therefore, in order to be balanced and whole, we need to embrace both sides in our magical practice. The Grey Witch is someone who can often appear outspoken, while at the same time they might be described as aloof, standoffish and unfriendly. This is just part of their personality: if there is nothing to say, they will remain quiet.

STRENGTHS

A Grey Witch's strength lies in their power protection spells. They can cast a protective barrier for any loved one, near or far. These witches excel at animal protection spells, and although their pets such as cats may wander far and wide, no harm comes to them, and they always find their way home.

SIGNS YOU COULD BE A GREY WITCH

* You have an uncanny ability to know when someone, including yourself, has been hexed or cursed.

* When you enter a room, you can feel the atmosphere and can sense if there has been an argument or if someone has been talking about you behind your back.

* You can be happy one moment and then suddenly change to feeling down depending on who you are with.

* You can have a fiery temper and are easily riled.

* You do not shy away or back down from a fight, even if it's to your detriment.

* You are fiercely loyal to those you love, including animals and pets.

THE CLOAK OF MIRRORS INVOCATION SPELL

The Cloak of Mirrors is an old spell. In ancient times, mirrors were held to have their own unique magical power, and were often used in divination spells. The Grey Witch, however, utilises the power of the mirror for protection and defensive magic. The Cloak of Mirrors protection spell works on the basis that if anything or anyone sends negativity to you, the bad intentions will bounce right off your mirrored cloak and go back to the person who sent them.

If you feel you need protection, then invoke the power of mirrors with this spell. On a full moon or when the moon is waxing (growing), stand in front of a mirror, safely holding a white candle with both hands. Say to your reflection:

> **I call upon the sacred power**
> **Of mirror magic, and upon this hour**
> **I invoke thine mirror cloak.**
> **I invoke, I invoke, I invoke.**
> **Come now and protect me**
> **From all those who would harm me.**
> **A mirror cloak now covers me.**
> **All negativities return to thee.**
> **From head to toe and all around,**
> **My safety and protection abound.**

Then blow out the candle and waft the smoke all around you. As you do so, imagine the rising smoke creating the Cloak of Mirrors all around you, covering your feet, legs, body, arms and head. This is your protection Cloak of Mirrors; wear it well and keep it for as long as you need it.

THE RED WITCH

CHARACTER
Loving, sympathetic,
kind-hearted, affectionate

LUCKY COLOUR
Red

LUCKY ANIMAL
Salamander

MAGICAL PRACTICE
Love charms and potions; spells for love,
friendships, sex and marriage,
love and harmony magic

DESCRIPTION

The Red Witch can also be called the Love Witch. This title does not only concern love between two consenting adults; it also refers to the love of friends, family and animals. The Red Witch is a wonderful purveyor of all manner of spells, potions, charms and brews that help, heal and guide us in all relationships and friendships. Their abilities are second to none when it comes to helping with matters concerning love and sex magic, or friends falling out, or siblings or even pets not getting along. The Red Witch is the magical practitioner of the heart par excellence.

STRENGTHS

The Red Witch's strength is their ability to feel and experience love in all its many forms. They feel love but can also give and send out love to one and all who need it. Their love charms and potions are incredibly powerful and can last a lifetime.

SIGNS YOU COULD BE A RED WITCH

* You feel emotions, especially love, very intensely, so much so that you could be an empath.

* You love to be in love and are only truly happy when you are caring for someone.

* You fall in love very easily and often, which can lead others to view you as promiscuous.

* You also love to be surrounded by beautiful things and have exquisite taste.

* You enjoy having fresh flowers everywhere in your home.

FRIENDS FALLEN OUT SPELL

If you long for the renewal of a friendship that has taken a turn for the worse, then cast this spell on a Wednesday night.

You'll need a picture of you and your friend or friends; it's OK if the picture is on your phone. Place the photo or phone in the centre of a table and surround it with red tealight candles: one red candle for each of your friends, including you. As you light the candles, say these words:

> **You and I were friends, as close as can be,**
> **But now you are nothing more than my frenemy.**
> **Renew our friendship, I ask of you.**
> **Let our bond never be broken if this**
> **friendship be true.**

Sit for a while watching the candles and remember all the good times you've had together. If the flames flicker, your spell has been heard – but if a candle suddenly goes out, the friendship is not meant to be renewed.

THE GREEN WITCH

CHARACTER
Natural, honest, open, communicative

LUCKY COLOUR
Green

LUCKY ANIMAL
Horse

MAGICAL PRACTICE
Earth magic, spells, plant power,
herb and flower magic

DESCRIPTION

The Green Witch, in many ways, is the eco-warrior of the witches. Green Witches are powerful defenders of the earth and will be the first ones on the scene if a forest, tree or green space is threatened by destruction. This witch deeply feels the devastation of the earth, and is angered by the pollution and lack of respect shown to nature. The Green Witch's strength and power stems from their ability to connect with all the forces of nature to bring about their desired results. This witch is no stranger to harvesting summer seeds, collecting spring rain when there is a rainbow, storing winter icicles in their freezer to be used as wands, or wishing on falling leaves in autumn. Every season, the Green Witch gleans a new resource from the earth to use in their magical practice.

STRENGTHS

The main strength of the Green Witch is their botanical knowledge; they know every tree in the forest and every wildflower growing in the meadow. Their gardens, if they are lucky enough to have them, are home to some of the strangest-looking plants you can find, as well as many types of herbs. If they do not have a garden, then every room in the house will be filled with plants, all of which will be healthy and have a purpose.

SIGNS YOU COULD BE A GREEN WITCH

✳ You're always collecting nature scraps when you go for a walk, such as pine cones, stones, tree bark and twigs.

✳ As a child, you checked to see if you liked butter by holding a buttercup under your chin, or blew dandelion seeds everywhere, or made daisy chains for hours – and you still do now.

✳ You also tried to make perfume with water and rose petals.

✳ You make your own teas from the different leaves, flowers and berries you collect.

✳ You have lots of houseplants that are always healthy and never die.

WINTER FLOWERS PREPARATION SPELL

The Green Witch loves all seasons, but is particularly drawn to the winter months, probably because they know that the earth is sleeping but literally bursting with life. Therefore, planting bulbs for the spring and summer becomes a favourite pastime, one upon which the Green Witch can place lots of magical intentions. Although it may still be bright in the evenings and days may still be warm, autumn brings with it a sense of preparation for winter, and we feel this in the garden as early spring bulbs need to be planted by now. Planting bulbs for the late winter festival of Imbolc is ideally done in autumn, especially if you are planting to grow the white snowdrops that symbolise the Goddess in her maiden form.

In September, preferably on the autumn equinox, plant snowdrop bulbs in a plant pot. As you plant your bulbs, say these words:

**For three months or more sleep tight,
As you go to bed in the September light.
When you awaken in the dark, your sleepy heads
Will grow and stretch, arriving in winter beds.
I am preparing for the festivals of winter rest.**

Make sure to lovingly tend to your bulbs and keep them outside, as they need the winter weather, the cold frosts and snow, to grow. We might think these flowers of early spring are delicate, but nothing could be further from the truth; the flowers that bloom in late winter are the toughest plants around, and remind us that we too can survive all that nature can throw at us.

THE WHITE WITCH

CHARACTER
Caring, compassionate,
empathetic, idealistic

LUCKY COLOUR
White

LUCKY ANIMAL
Caterpillar

MAGICAL PRACTICE
Spiritual guidance, spells for the greater
good, potions and good luck charms,
visualisation and manifestation magic

DESCRIPTION

White Witches are the powerful warriors for the greater good. They feel injustices strongly and will always aim to do the 'right' thing, even if it is detrimental to themselves. They are fiercely loyal and will defend the less confident at a moment's notice. They are great colleagues and friends, and will always be on your side if you face difficulties. There is nothing that infuriates these witches more than prejudice and injustice. Although their magic is for the greater good and benefit of all, they are not averse to being a force to be reckoned with if there has been wrongdoing.

STRENGTHS

A White Witch's greatest strength is their passion for the 'right' thing. They are aware of their own power and confidence, and aim to use both for the benefit of all. They do not seek fame or fortune for their good actions. These witches certainly do not lack the courage of their convictions; they are fiercely strong and are unafraid to do battle alone if needs be.

SIGNS YOU COULD BE A WHITE WITCH

✴ You feel extremely passionate if there has been an injustice done to your friends or family.

✴ You detest prejudice in any form.

✴ You value honesty and transparency above everything.

✴ You seek to be the best version of yourself.

✴ You have an innate desire to make the world better on every level.

✴ You always get picked to be on teams, as people want you on their side.

FULL MOON HONESTY CHARM

Honesty is a beautiful virtue that at times seems to be missing from our daily lives. You may experience dishonesty from people in different areas of your life, from work colleagues to lovers and friends, or even children and family members. As a White Witch, nothing would infuriate you more than lack of honesty in people. The full moon is a moon that commands nothing but the truth from all who catch her gaze.

If there is an area of your life where honesty is lacking, create an honesty charm and hang it in the place where lies and dishonesty appear the most.

On the night of a pure, white full moon, take a small white cloth bag, and place inside some fennel, a sprig of lavender, one star anise and a small silver moon charm or a small picture of the moon. Tie it closed with a white ribbon. As you tie it, say:

> **Show me the truth of spoken words.**
> **Let me always be aware.**
> **Grant me the gift and speciality,**
> **Of knowing the true honesty.**
> **Wherever this little bag goes,**
> **Truth and honesty now flow.**

Hang up the bag where you feel it is needed the most, from the office to the kitchen – anywhere you think honesty is needed and may be absent.

THE BLUE WITCH

CHARACTER
Psychic, wise, healing, spiritual

LUCKY COLOUR
Blue

LUCKY ANIMAL
Dolphin

MAGICAL PRACTICE
Healing tonics, meditation
practices, potions and brews,
meditation magic and healing potions

DESCRIPTION

A relative newcomer to types of witches, this new witch is emerging in a world of pain. Their ultimate aim is the healing of people, animals and the earth itself. Although the Green Witch is responsible for the physical earth in general, the Blue Witch's primary concern is the healing of the planet from all the years of hurt, devastation and pain. The Blue Witch is therefore a healer of the soul, the spiritual and the sacred. The Blue Witch is also the healer of the mind, and they make great counsellors and therapists.

STRENGTHS

The strength of the Blue Witch is their innate ability to know exactly how someone feels. There is no hiding emotions or worries with these witches, as they can literally feel your pain. They have the strength to heal you and can listen to your concerns for hours. Their magical strength is the healing of mind, body and soul, for these witches are acutely aware of the connection between psyche and soma. They know that what we think and feel can affect the body in both positive and negative ways, and their spells and potions aim to heal holistically.

SIGNS YOU COULD BE A BLUE WITCH

✴ You care deeply for others.

✴ You are a highly attuned empath.

✴ You cannot bear to see another living being in pain.

✴ You experience physical pain when there has been an environmental disaster.

✴ People always come to you with their problems – you are the group's agony aunt/uncle.

SPRING MOON AWAKENING BODY TONIC

The Blue Witch is all about healing holistically, and knows that toxins carried within can lead to complications. This witch will have a ritual cleanse every season, beginning with a 'spring clean' of the body. You can cleanse your body with the help of plants including spring nettles, herbs and dandelions, to name but a few. These plants can renew our energy and detox the body of toxins accumulated throughout the long winter months of possible overeating and indulgence. Harvest these in the spring moonlight if you can for an extra kick of power, especially the nettles.

Harvest nettles wearing gloves, then wash and flash-boil in boiling water for 3–5 minutes to remove the sting. You can then use them or cook with them as you would spinach.

INGREDIENTS

50 g (1¾ oz) prepared nettles, 50 g (1¾ oz) lemon balm leaves, 1 pint of water, 2 tablespoons honey

METHOD

Combine all the ingredients in a saucepan and bring to the boil. After about 5 minutes, remove from the heat and allow to steep for at least an hour, then strain the mixture through a sieve, so you are left with a clear liquid. Discard the nettles and lemon balm leaves. Pour the liquid into a bottle and leave it overnight in the spring moonlight. In the morning, drink a good glassful with your breakfast; you can serve it with lemon slices and some ice if it's a warm spring day.

As you drink the tonic, say this spell:

**Awaken body, awaken soul.
Embrace the cleansing and vitality,
Powering up on the Moon's energy.**

NATURE
WITCHES

The world of nature witches features some of the
most powerful environmentally aware witches.
Although all these witches hold nature and the earth
in their hearts, they individually bring a unique focus,
such as the Sea Witch, who specifically cares for
and utilises the power of the oceans and seas in their
magic, or the Weather Witch, who draws their magic
from all types of weather, including all the strange
and wonderful weather phenomena we encounter.
Enjoy the wonderful world of nature witches.

A storm has been predicted. You:

a. feel tingly with excitement
b. rush to the coast to check out the waves
c. close all windows and doors and stay inside
d. put out buckets and plastic bowls to catch as much rainwater as possible
e. watch the storm through the windows

Your ideal vacation is:

a. skiing with plenty of sports
b. by the sea or on a boat
c. visiting historical places
d. exploring nature, such as waterfalls
e. something of geological importance, like looking for crystals

Your ideal garden is one with lots of:

a. patios and shelter, like a gazebo
b. water features
c. plants and trees with a splendid lawn
d. flowers, water features, stone formations and a fire pit or barbecue
e. plants in pots, a rockery, stepping stones set in gravel

What is your ideal plant?

a. oak tree
b. water lily
c. rose bush
d. hyacinth
e. no plants – they always die with me

What is your favourite crystal?

a. sapphire
b. aquamarine
c. amethyst
d. ruby
e. quartz

You prefer to be:

a. in between sea and countryside
b. in the sea
c. overlooking the sea
d. on the sea
e. on the beach

You have got a lazy weekend planned. You intend to:

a. watch the clouds
b. spend hours in the bathroom
c. cook some meals for the coming week
d. sleep, eat, watch Netflix, and sleep some more
e. spend hours in the garden

You like to eat:

a. barbecues/picnic foods
b. sushi and fish dishes
c. traditional dishes, like Sunday roasts
d. spicy foods, like curries
e. sweet dishes, like puddings and ice cream

Your favourite celebrations are:

a. birthdays
b. summer vacations
c. Christmas
d. Halloween
e. weddings

MOSTLY AS: WEATHER WITCH

The Weather Witch is a witch of the weather. They focus on and harness the energies of whatever type of weather is prevalent, but a thunderstorm is their preference. As such, the Weather Witch can also be called the Storm Witch.

MOSTLY BS: SEA WITCH

The Sea Witch is a witch who not only loves to be by the sea but any form of water, such as rivers, streams, lakes, lochs, ponds and even fountains. These witches find magic in any body of water and draw their magical energy from it. Sea Witches can live anywhere, in cities or out in the countryside, but there will always be water nearby, even if it's just a goldfish bowl or a water feature in the home.

MOSTLY CS: TRADITIONAL WITCH

As the name implies, the wonderful Traditional Witch is very traditional and set in their ways - at times to their detriment. Yet the wise age-old beliefs and ways to which they adhere can be a lesson to us all. These witches have knowledge of every aspect of witchcraft, and their strength is in traditional ways of magic, such as spells and potions.

MOSTLY DS: ELEMENTAL WITCH

The Elemental Witch is a master of the elements and will use the powers of earth, air, fire and water in all areas of their magic. These are the witches who will be deeply connected to the pentagram and will use it in their practice with correspondences (see A Witch's Dictionary on page 139 for more of an explanation).

MOSTLY ES: JEWEL WITCH

The Jewel Witch is a witch who is not only a purveyor of crystals but all-powerful stones, metals and fossils as well. They are deeply fascinated by the origins of stones and their geological history. They are also avid palaeontologists, who love to find and harness the power of fossils and ancient stonework, and they are aware of the energies contained within mosaics.

THE WEATHER WITCH

CHARACTER
Powerful, forceful, independent, intense

LUCKY COLOUR
Silver

LUCKY ANIMAL
Robin

MAGICAL PRACTICE
Weather manifestation spells,
cloud divination, storm spells

DESCRIPTION

Weather Witches are renowned for their weather manifestation spells.
These witches can create storms, rain, rainbows, snow and sunshine.
They are adept at reading the signs of cloud formations, and regularly
use cloud divination in their practice. They are always looking up,
because they are watching the clouds and seeing the answers in them.
However, their most powerful form of magic stems from creating
storms and harnessing the energy that is contained within them.
Their favourite time of year is when the Thunder Moon is on the
horizon, and they will do a lot of their magical work during this month.

STRENGTHS

These witches love a good storm. They are not afraid to be out in
a thunderstorm and will draw down the energy contained within
the storm by putting out copious amounts of containers to collect
rainwater. This thunder water, as it is sometimes known, is then used
in spells, potions and brews to create a powerful addition to anything
magical. Weather Witches also collect rainbow water, which is the rain
that falls during a rainbow.

SIGNS YOU COULD BE A WEATHER WITCH

✦ You love to use any gifts the weather gives, such as snapping
off icicles and storing them in the freezer to use as wands.

✦ You have lots of pots and containers so you can capture
rainwater or thunder water.

✦ You are always watching the weather forecast, and have
a weather app on your phone.

✦ You feel tingly when the first snow arrive.

✦ You jump for joy when you see a rainbow, and get a real
buzz from a summer shower.

THUNDER MOON POWER-UP MY CAREER SPELL

If your work seems to have stalled and you feel you are going nowhere with your chosen career path, and you want to know whether you should leave or stick it out, gather the rain from a thunderstorm and keep it to use in this career spell.

On the night of the Thunder Moon, sprinkle some salt on a flat surface, like a tray or table, and then, with your index finger, write your career or job title in the salt. Sit back and look at it, and feel the emotions that come up concerning your job. Then, when you are ready, say these words:

> **Thunder Moon of Power, I ask of you:**
> **My career is stuck like glue,**
> **Nothing seems to move at all.**
> **Should I quit and will I fall?**
> **Thunder Moon, power up my fate.**
> **Help my career before it's too late.**

Now, sprinkle some of the thunder water on the salt word and see what happens. If the word remains, then it is a sign to stay with the job. If the word seems to dissipate and melt away, then it is time to leave the job and seek pastures new.

THE SEA WITCH

CHARACTER
Changeable, flexible,
protective, secretive

LUCKY COLOUR
Turquoise

LUCKY ANIMAL
Frog

MAGICAL PRACTICE
Spells, potions and brews, any magical
practice with liquid at its core, water
magic and scrying with water

DESCRIPTION

The Sea Witch has power over all water, including ponds and fountains. Anywhere there is a body of water, no matter its purpose, this witch governs. The Sea Witch is also very changeable in nature, just like the sea; one moment they can be calm, and in another they can whip up into an almighty frenzy. Their magic is centred around water, and if they have an altar, it will be one that includes a water feature.

STRENGTHS

Sea Witches are very much in touch with their emotions, but they can go to extremes; for example, they can become overprotective of their loved ones. However, although they can be over the top, the power of their emotions is one of the strengths of the Sea Witch. They can be incredibly protective over the ocean and seas and, like the Green Witch, they are passionate about protecting these environments; they are ocean warriors. They are especially concerned with pollution and the plastics that are now found in the seas, oceans and rivers of our world. As such, they focus their strength on active spells for cleansing the emotions and cleaning the oceans.

SIGNS YOU COULD BE A SEA WITCH

★ You have a sudden, changeable nature, but you are also very flexible and can easily adapt to any situation.

★ You are incredibly intuitive.

★ You sometimes have dreams and visions that come true.

★ You like to collect seashells, sea glass, driftwood and basically anything that the tide washes up, but you never take more than is needed, and you always remember that seashells are also homes for sea animals.

★ You go with the flow of life.

WATER CLEANSING SPELL

One of the main types of spells Sea Witches perform regularly is a water cleansing spell. It can be performed anywhere and everywhere, and is for any kind of water, including a dirty river or stream.

The main ingredient is a glass jar or bottle full of water from the body of water you wish to cleanse; for example, if it is the sea, then collect some sea water when you are at the beach. If you are in the countryside or city and there is a dirty river nearby, then safely collect some water from it. You only need enough to fill one glass jam jar or a small glass bottle.

Line a sieve or colander with a coffee filter or a piece of muslin, then place this over a clean glass bowl. Pour your sea water or dirty river water into the sieve or colander and allow it to drip through to the clean bowl. As you pour, say these words:

> **Cleansed and pure**, **filtered through.**
> **I will cleanse the oceans/sea/river**
> (*delete as appropriate*) **blue.**
> **No more the plastic and toxic waste.**
> **Rubbish now disperse from this space.**
> **Brother ocean and sister sea,**
> **Please forgive humanity.**

Repeat this filtering process three times, changing the muslin cloth or coffee filter each time. Then pour the water back into the glass jar or bottle, make sure you have washed out the container before filling it with the cleansed water. Pour this cleansed water back into the sea or river you collected it from so it can work its magic.

THE TRADITIONAL WITCH

CHARACTER
Conventional, conformist,
unadventurous, routine-loving

LUCKY COLOUR
Brown

LUCKY ANIMAL
Ant

MAGICAL PRACTICE
Traditional spells, rituals and potions,
has excellent knowledge of the
correspondences, any form of
correspondence magic

DESCRIPTION

The Traditional Witch has excellent knowledge of the correspondences (see A Witch's Dictionary on page 139 for an explanation). This witch will make sure to learn all the correspondences in the universe so they know how everything connects. For example, they will know that spells for love or wealth are best cast on a Friday under a waxing moon, using green candles and basil. They will know these things almost instinctively, and will weave all corresponding items together into a powerful magical spell. They will certainly have an altar and will use it throughout their daily magical practices. It will be adorned with all the traditional items, such as candles, a mini cauldron, incense, an athame, a black-handled sharp knife, a bit like a kitchen knife and a pentagram or pentacle.

STRENGTHS

A Traditional Witch is, as the name suggests, very traditional in their magical practice. They will follow the Wheel of the Year and will likely particularly enjoy Midsummer or the Summer Solstice. Their magic weaves all the correspondences together and their spells are very powerful.

SIGNS YOU COULD BE A TRADITIONAL WITCH

✴ You like routine and do not like anything too adventurous.

✴ You read copious amounts of published grimoires or spell books.

✴ You're interested in joining a coven.

✴ You have many sets of different-coloured candles.

✴ You tend to be very organised.

MIDSUMMER MOON INCENSE SPELL

A traditional witch will work with all the magic around herb, especially on certain nights of the year, and Midsummer or the Summer Solstice is probably one of their favourite times to create magic, especially making incense. There are two ways of making incense and one is easier than the other. This is the easy one as the ingredients are readily available and easy to find.

INGREDIENTS

1 charcoal block, selection of dried herbs such as lavender for love, rosemary for health, mint for luck, basil for wealth

METHOD

Grind all the herbs together in a pestle and mortar until they become really small. Then light the charcoal block and allow it to start crackling away. Take three pinches of your herb mixture, sprinkle on top of the charcoal and allow the rising smoke to infuse through the herbs.

As you add the three pinches say these words:

> **Midsummer magic, Midsummer light,**
> **I cast upon this magical night.**
> **Midsummer moon I ask of you,**
> **Grant me wishes that are true.**
> **Incense herbs of might,**
> **I cast these wishes when alight.**

Then enjoy the Midsummer night and cast your wishes and watch the rising incense smoke carry your wishes up to the universe.

THE ELEMENTAL WITCH

CHARACTER
Concise, realistic, grounded, decisive

LUCKY COLOUR
Olive

LUCKY ANIMAL
Bumblebee

MAGICAL PRACTICE
Elemental magic, using the four traditional
elements of earth, air, fire and water

MAGICAL SPECIALITY
Elemental seasonal spells

DESCRIPTION

The Elemental Witch has power over the traditional elements of earth, air, fire and water, but they will also recognise the fifth element of spirit, divinity or the universe. This witch will certainly have an altar, and each element will be represented: a chalice or cup for water, incense for air, a candle for fire, and a plant or little pot of soil for earth. The fifth element of spirit will be represented by their chosen deity, a god or goddess, or they will simply choose to adhere to the universe. This witch will also know the elemental power of salt, as this wonderful gift encompasses all the elements. Salt can be mined from deep underground; therefore, it is earth. Salt can also come from the sea, which, of course, is water, and both mined salt and sea salt are dried in the air. Finally, if you put a grain of salt on your tongue, it burns; thus, it is also fire. Therefore, salt is the one sacred ingredient we have in this world that encompasses all the four elements. The Elemental Witch will know this, for they will have a little bowl of salt on their altar too.

STRENGTHS

An Elemental Witch's strength may lie in their ability to cast spells using all four elements, or they may specialise in just one. This witch is a master of the elements and seeks to utilise energy in all its many forms in their magical practice, whether they are specialising in one element or all.

SIGNS YOU COULD BE AN ELEMENTAL WITCH

✷ You believe in the elementals of nature – yep, you believe in fairies.

✷ You like to go for walks on windy days, and say thank you to the element of air.

✷ You love the elemental magic that each season brings: summer brings sun (fire); autumn brings wind (air); winter brings rain and snow (water), and spring brings plants and flowers (earth).

✷ You have representatives of each element throughout your home.

60

WINTER MOON HEALING SNOW SPELL

An Elemental Witch will love the power of change each season brings, and will harness this energy for a range of spells. If there has been a good fall of fresh snow and the moon beams are shining right on it, then collect a small amount of this snow to make a healing elixir. As you scoop up the moonbeam in the snow, say these words over it:

> **Earth, air, fire and water might,**
> **I catch the falling snow of moonbeam light.**
> **I catch your strength with all my might.**
> **Heal my aching body and mind.**
> **Your healing powers merge with mine.**
> **Earth, air, fire and water, make it right.**

Collect the snow in a jar or a bowl, transfer it into a small saucepan and melt it over a low heat. Pour the melted snow into a bottle, then label and date it, and use within the season. To use, pour some of your melted snow into a bath or add it to your shower gel. Add a pinch of salt, too, to represent all the elements, then wash yourself with the healing snow beam.

THE JEWEL WITCH

CHARACTER
Scientific, analytical,
sensitive, visual

LUCKY COLOUR
Gold

LUCKY ANIMAL
Dragonfly

MAGICAL PRACTICE
Crystal magic, crystal wand
spells and crystal potions

MAGICAL SPECIALITY
Crystal elixirs

DESCRIPTION

Many people find their way into witchcraft via their love of crystals, but a Jewel Witch is not just a lover of shiny objects. The Jewel Witch will have a deep connection to these powerful rocks, which resonate with the energy of the earth that created them. This witch will also be rather scientific as a consequence, and will love to learn about how crystals, metals and fossils are formed. The Jewel Witch will study formations of thousands of years, learning how volcanic eruptions, tree sap and the meteors that crash into our planet can become crystals and fossils such as moldavite, quartz and amber. These wonderful rocks and metals hold a power over the Jewel Witch, who uses them in all their magical practice, from spells to elixirs to the mixing of crystal-infused sugar and salt.

STRENGTHS

Jewel Witches have an innate sense of which crystal, stone or metal will help and heal in any situation. For example, they will be the first to suggest gently rubbing a stye with a gold ring - but only gold. Their knowledge on how you can use crystals is second to none, and they regularly charge their crystals, as they know that magic is energy and energy transforms and transcends from one source to another. For example, when 'charging' crystals by leaving them in the moonlight, the powerful moon rays transcend and infuse the crystal with lunar energy, making the stone extra powerful.

SIGNS YOU COULD BE A JEWEL WITCH

✦ Your home is full of crystals and marble.

✦ You have lots of crystal, gold and silver jewellery.

✦ You collect fossils.

✦ You have a crystal on your key ring and probably one in your car.

✦ You may own an unusual amount of gold and silver-coloured clothes and shoes.

GOLDEN WATER SPELL

The Jewel Witch knows the power of crystal water on the mind, body and soul, but they will also be aware of the benefits of gold water. Crystal water is more commonly called an elixir and is easily made by popping your desired crystals, such as quartz or amethyst, in a bottle of water and leaving in the fridge overnight. Always remove the crystals before drinking. A word of warning, though: please always check what crystal you are using, as not all crystals can be used this way. Some crystals are porous and some are toxic, such as Vanadinite, so please be cautious of how you use your crystals.

Although metal water is not ingested as it can be toxic, gold water is very beneficial when used as a blessing water around the house or even in your place of work.

On a sunny day (ideally a Sunday), place a piece of gold jewellery in a bottle of water, then pop in the sunlight for no more than ten minutes. Let the sun's rays penetrate the bottle, infusing it with energy and power. Now carefully remove the jewellery and pour the gold water into a spray bottle. Add three pinches of salt to the water, then pop on the lid, and shake the bottle while saying these words:

> **The gold of earth has blessed you.**
> **The power of the sun has caressed you.**
> **I invoke you now to wake.**
> **Release your energies, success to make.**

This golden water can now be used to enhance success. If you are working on a project for work or school, spray some round your desk to bring about a successful result.

MYSTICAL WITCHES

The different worlds or realms are where the esoteric and mystical witches reside, from the ethereal qualities of the Fae Witch to the outer-world powers of the Cosmic Witch. These witches are the ones who literally have stars in their eyes, and although physically they are very much earthbound, their magical practices – and hearts, for that matter – are certainly not. These witches will call upon energies from different realms of existence to help them with their magic, and their spells will encompass all the power of the universe. Here, you will encounter an array of magical beings and esoteric practices, from tarot to tea reading. Welcome to the world of mystical, magical, magnificent witches.

Your favourite mythical beings are:

a. goddesses
b. aliens
c. dragons
d. angels
e. fairies

Your favourite astral body planet is:

a. the moon
b. the sun
c. all of them
d. Saturn
e. Neptune

You get along mostly with:

a. water signs: Pisces, Cancer, Scorpio
b. air signs: Libra, Gemini, Aquarius
c. fire signs: Sagittarius, Aries, Leo
d. earth signs: Taurus, Virgo, Capricorn
e. everyone

Your favourite time of day is:

a. night-time
b. early morning – dawn
c. evening – dusk
d. daytime – noon
e. anytime is fine by me

Your favourite celestial event is:

a. eclipse
b. spring equinox
c. autumn equinox
d. midwinter
e. Midsummer

Your favourite form of divination is:

a. scrying with a bowl of water or mirror
b. tarot cards/runes
c. oracle cards
d. tasseomancy (reading tea leaves)
e. flower reading/Ogham

Your favourite film genre is:

a. romance
b. sci-fi
c. action
d. comedy
e. fantasy

Your ideal recreational sport would be:

a. hot air ballooning
b. mountaineering/rock-climbing
c. cycling
d. skydiving
e. swimming/canoeing

Your ideal holiday destination is:

a. China/Japan
b. Tenerife/Australia
c. Scandinavia
d. USA/Mexico
e. Ireland/Scotland/Wales

Your favourite fairy tale is:

a. *Cinderella*
b. *The Elves and the Shoemaker*
c. *Snow White and the Seven Dwarves*
d. *The Princess and the Pea*
e. *The Little Mermaid*

MOSTLY AS: LUNAR WITCH

The Lunar Witch is a witch whose magical practice revolves around the moon. This is the witch who knows every phase and every quarter of the lunar cycle. The Lunar Witch has spells and rituals for every type of moon, from Blue Moons to Blood Moons to Strawberry Moons.

MOSTLY BS: COSMIC WITCH

A Cosmic Witch is very much a witch of the sky, and they will focus on the energies of the universe. The Cosmic Witch will harness the energies of eclipses, equinoxes, stars and supernovas. For them, all the universe is deeply connected to the earth.

MOSTLY CS: ZODIAC WITCH

The Zodiac Witch practises magic in relation to the zodiac, and not just their own birth chart. They are adept at utilising the connections and characteristics of the zodiac for their magical practice, which will include reading charts and knowing the right times to manifest things. Their spells will always contain references to the zodiac signs, and they will cast at the right time for a particular star sign.

MOSTLY DS: DIVINATION WITCH

A Divination Witch will have a veritable supply of tarot cards, scrying bowls and wands. They are witches with such power for knowing the future that at times they can be guilty of thinking too much about tomorrow and not enough about today.

MOSTLY ES: FAE WITCH

The Fae Witch is an elemental practitioner of the Craft, and they will work with the energies of Fae, including all magical beings, such as dragons, mermaids and especially elves. These witches are the true innocent practitioners of the Craft. However, don't mistake their gentle appearance for being a sign that they are a pushover; just remember they also use dragon fire magic.

THE LUNAR WITCH

CHARACTER
Mysterious, beguiling, emotional, moody

LUCKY COLOUR
Lilac

LUCKY ANIMAL
Owl

MAGICAL PRACTICE
Moon magic par excellence,
phases of the moon
correspondence magic

DESCRIPTION

The Lunar Witch has such a powerful connection to the moon that they must be allowed to look at the moon at least once a week. Their magic is influenced by the stages of the moon, and they will know instinctively if the moon is waxing or waning. They will know that waxing is good for growing and manifesting things, as this is precisely what the moon is doing in this phase, while waning means diminishing, which is perfect for taking away things or getting rid of something, such as a bad habit. Lunar Witches will also have an altar outside if possible, and will prefer to do their magic underneath the white glare of the moon.

STRENGTHS

Lunar Witches' strengths lie in their ability to create very potent spells and potions using resources that have been infused with the power of the moon, such as moon salt or moon water. It is very easy to make moon water or moon salt; all you need is the salt or water and the full moon. On the night of the full moon, place your salt or water in the light of the moon and leave until the morning. Afterwards, safely store and label, and use as needed. However, a Lunar Witch will not just make moon water or moon salt; they will have a veritable cupboard of resources infused with moon rays, including oils, crystals, herbs that have been harvested in the glow of the moon, and much more.

SIGNS YOU COULD BE A LUNAR WITCH

✴ You feel compelled to look at the moon, even through glass.

✴ You instinctively know if the moon is waxing or waning.

✴ You know the name of each month's full moon.

✴ You prefer to practise magic outside, underneath the moon.

✴ You are a night person, as you feel you 'come alive' at night and find it difficult to sleep

MOONTONE 528 LOVE SPELL

The moon is not just a dead satellite circling around Earth; it is alive with energy and power, and also resonates its own frequency. The moon resonates at 528hz, which is the same frequency as what is known as the Love Frequency. The Love Frequency was used by ancient healers, priests and monks, who would tune their instruments to, and sing and chant at, this frequency. The Love Frequency become known as the Moontone.

The Moontone is often regarded as the miracle tone, as it is used to help restore, rebalance and realign the mind, body and spirit. It is regarded as the most special of all Solfeggio frequencies. Solfeggio frequencies are a part of a six-tone scale that can be found in many forms of music, such as Gregorian chanting and other forms of meditative music.

Using the Moontone, we can create a powerful love spell by pairing it with the herb fennel. Fennel can be used to increase sexual desire and boost the libido. There are plenty of places online where you can listen to the Moontone while casting this spell.

While playing the Moontone in the background. Write your intended love's name on a piece of paper in red ink and sprinkle fennel seeds over it while saying:

Together, my love and me,
Embracing our sexuality,
Loving unconditionally,
Together in sweet harmony.

Meditate on the music for a while and feel the power of the Moontone. Fold the paper with the seeds inside and keep it in a safe location. After the spell has played out, and you have achieved your goal, scatter the seeds in the garden.

THE COSMIC WITCH

CHARACTER
Open-minded, expansive,
energetic, scientific

LUCKY COLOUR
Indigo

LUCKY ANIMAL
Spider

MAGICAL PRACTICE
Utilises cosmic energy in their practice,
such as the energy of comets,
meteors and supernovas,
eclipse magic

DESCRIPTION

Cosmic Witches are amazing; they harness the power of the cosmos in each spell they cast and every potion they brew. They are particularly good at charms, and make sure to harness the energy of planetary alignments and passing meteor showers or comets in their magical work. These witches know everything there is to know about the cosmos. They will be aware of comets, black holes, planets, asteroids and galaxies. They will also be rather scientific and will like watching the night sky. They will probably have been to at least one observatory and will know the best places to view the universe with the naked eye.

STRENGTHS

Cosmic Witches pack a pretty powerful punch when they need to. These witches are very good at harnessing cosmic powers to eliminate a hex or curse. They can remove anything, including negative energies that may be haunting you or your house, as Cosmic Witches are also aware of multidimensional realms and the beings that manifest within them. As such, these witches know exactly how to send them right back to where they belong.

Eclipses are wonderful cosmic events. A Cosmic Witch will utilise these cosmic gifts through their practice either by making a specific eclipse candle for an eclipse ritual or by casting spells, creating charms or making incense according to the particular eclipse.

SIGNS YOU COULD BE A COSMIC WITCH

✴ You like sci-fi films.

✴ You have a telescope for watching the night sky.

✴ You have a star chart or a diary featuring the cosmos.

✴ You know when the next comet will appear in the sky.

✴ You know when each of the annual meteor showers begins.

BANISHING CHARM

Create a banishing charm when someone or something has difficulty understanding that enough is enough. A banishing charm can be made from anything that particular person has given you: a ring, a necklace, a bracelet or anything at all. If they have never given you anything, create a little drawstring bag with three pinches of sage, one pinch of cumin and a photo of them. As you wind the ribbon around the photo or gift, say:

I call upon the universe,
To stop your deeds or worse.
I banish you from ever doing harm.
I banish you, but will not harm.
I banish you, I banish you.
Stay away from those I love too.

Hang the object or bag in a place where that person used to be, but out of view – perhaps hidden in a plant, or high up in the corner. If at work, keep it in your desk drawer. A banishing charm is stronger when is made utlising the power of the eclipse.

ECLIPSE CORRESPONDENCE CHART

Eclipse	Oil	Colour	Herb	Plants
Lunar	Opium	Indigo	Wormwood	Dragon's blood
Solar	Neroli	Black	Rue	Mandrake

THE ZODIAC WITCH

CHARACTER
Mathematical, statistical,
inquisitive, truthful

LUCKY COLOUR
Maroon

LUCKY ANIMAL
Hare

MAGICAL PRACTICE
Astrological magic, combining the star
signs' energies into spells and charms,
planetary magic

DESCRIPTION

The Zodiac Witch will know immediately what star sign someone is, and they will probably also know their moon sign. Zodiac Witches know the traits and characteristics of every one of the twelve astrological signs. A Zodiac Witch will also be familiar with all the different forms of zodiacs, not just ones that pertain to the West. For example, they will be familiar with the Chinese zodiac, Vedic Astrology and many other different types of zodiacs throughout history, such as ancient Egyptian. They may choose one to specialise in, or use all the different zodiacs to enhance their magical practice.

STRENGTHS

The Zodiac Witch's strength lies in their ability to create a very potent charm, especially if they are using a piece of jewellery that has been given to someone on their birthday, which will make it extra potent. They are also able to weave correspondences into a bracelet, such as a friendship bracelet, to protect the wearer, and they can weave the energies of a person's ruling planet into a charm for good luck, protection and love. Such is their knowledge of the planets and their place in the heavens that they will cast their spells and charms when the planet is on the ascendant within the night sky.

SIGNS YOU COULD BE A ZODIAC WITCH

✦ You have your own birth chart and study how to create birth charts.

✦ You know someone's star sign within minutes of meeting them.

✦ You know your friends' star signs, and know which ones can keep a secret (Scorpios are the best at keeping secrets).

✦ You know every month by its star signs, e.g., January is Capricorn, February is Aquarius, March is Pisces and Aries, and so on.

ZODIAC CHARM

The Zodiac Charm is a piece of jewellery which is intended for a particular person and can be used on anything, such as a key ring, phone or bag. The time and energy the Zodiac Witch spends making it ensures that this becomes a very potent charm. All the resources require the recipient's star sign. For example, let's suppose the recipient is a Gemini. The ruling planet for Gemini is Mercury, which is seen in the early morning or early evening, so a Zodiac Witch would cast the charm during this time, preferably outdoors, when little Mercury can be seen. The colours of Gemini are yellows and blues, especially light blue, and the symbol of Gemini is the sign of the twins. Therefore, to make this Zodiac Charm, you would use three identical lengths of ribbon: one yellow, one light blue and one silver, as silver is the colour of Mercury. Have two identical objects to weave into it, such as two identical silver charms or two feathers or stones – whatever you like. Weave the three strands of ribbon together like a braid, attaching the charms as you go. As you weave, say these words:

I charm these ribbons of yellow, silver and blue.
I weave good luck, love and money just for you.
I weave the magic of Mercury too,
Of Gemini abundance in charms of two.

When you've finished, leave the charm out in the glare of Mercury until he disappears from the sky, then give it to your Gemini friend. Zodiac Charms made by a Zodiac Witch are all different depending on the recipient and their star sign, so adjust the colours and planet accordingly, and change the intentions of the spell to suit your specific requirements. As a Zodiac Witch, you have all the power within to easily perform this task.

THE DIVINATION WITCH

CHARACTER
Intuitive, knowledgeable,
clairsentient, psychic

LUCKY COLOUR
Yellow

LUCKY ANIMAL
Butterfly

MAGICAL PRACTICE
Divination, using tools such as
tarot cards, oracle cards, runes,
clouds and flowers, scrying

DESCRIPTION

A Divination Witch is a fascinating witch who can be everything
and anything for divination, which means seeing the future or the
unknown. These are the witches who will read tarot cards, oracle
cards, tea leaves, coffee grains, flowers, ribbons, playing cards –
basically absolutely anything and everything, including cloud formation
– in order to see the future or answer questions about the present.
These witches may also have spontaneous visions or prophetic dreams.
Indeed, they may perform most of their magical work using dreams
and/or while in a meditative state or trance.

STRENGTHS

There are many forms of divination, and the Divination Witch will
be talented in a specific one – or all of them. They could be especially
attuned to working with a particular form of divination due to their
environment. For example, depending on their surroundings, they
might use flowers, trees or even birds as their tool for prophecy.

SIGNS YOU COULD BE A DIVINATION WITCH

✳ You have dreams that come true.

✳ You know who is going to call you before the phone even rings.

✳ You've experienced many coincidences throughout your life,
such as thinking of someone you haven't seen in a long time
then suddenly meeting them.

✳ You may experience moments of déjà vu.

✳ You may look in the mirror but see a different reflection; this is
known as 'spontaneous scrying'. Scrying, as we'll see on the next
page, is a method of seeing the future using a reflective surface,
such as a mirror or a bowl of water, but you can also scry with
flames, so you may also see things in a candle flame.

SCRYING

One of the main types of divination is scrying. Begin by choosing your specific scrying tool. Place an unlit white candle, a black-bottomed bowl of water and a mirror side by side on a table. Close your eyes and, with open palms, run your hands over the objects, making sure not to touch them. When you feel a slight tingle or a sense of pressure or warmth in your hands or fingertips, then open your eyes to reveal the scrying tool with which you are most in tune. Use this tool for your scrying.

If you have chosen the candle, light it. If you have chosen the bowl of water or the mirror, position them in front of you. Write down any questions you may have on a piece of paper. Keep to closed questions initially, and then once you have grasped the basics of scrying, you can ask open questions. Examples of closed questions include 'is this job right for me?', 'am I on the right life path' and 'should I follow my dreams?' Hold the paper in both hands and meditate on it. As you do so, say these words:

I see I may, I see I might.
Show me now, what is right.

Open your eyes, and quickly and safely look into the candle flame, or into the mirror or bowl of water. You will probably see an image forming or experience flashes of images in your mind's eye. This is your answer.

You alone will be able to make sense of these images. As a Divination Witch, the meanings will come automatically to you.

THE FAE WITCH

CHARACTER
Imaginative, gentle, fun, flirty

LUCKY COLOUR
Fuchsia

LUCKY ANIMAL
Mouse

MAGICAL PRACTICE
Elemental energy magic: earth (gnomes/
fairies), air (angels), fire (salamanders/
Djinn) and water (mermaids/kelpies),
fae spells of sight and transformation

DESCRIPTION

The Fae Witch is one of the most mystical of all the different witch types. This witch regularly communes with all beings of the fairy realm. If they are lucky enough to have a garden, they will most likely have a special place for the 'wee folk' within it; if not, they will make sure to have a window box or patio planters full of flowers that fairies like. These witches are not afraid to invite fairies into their home, and will have little doors and welcome signs for them.

STRENGTHS

A Fae Witch is very good at wishing magic. They are particularly adept at making wishing bundles or wish boxes, as they are more commonly called. Wishing bundles are made from everyday objects and are intended to turn wishes and dreams into reality. They are very easy to make; simply collect items that represent your wish and pop them into a small box. For example, if you want a new job or a specific career, you might collect a picture of the uniform, a name tag, a briefcase – whatever items represent your desired job. Add a silver or gold candle, some flowers (preferably ones that have bells, such as bluebells), a real bell or bells (if you can), rose petals, pine cones, acorns, twigs, leaves or anything else from nature that is easily available. Wrap the box with some silver or gold ribbon and keep it somewhere safe until your wish comes to fruition.

SIGNS YOU COULD BE A FAE WITCH

✴ You may see flashes of light, like little sparks of silver and gold.

✴ You may feel cobwebs brushing your face when there are none.

✴ You may hear strange music or the sound of little bells.

✴ You may experience things going missing in your house, like keys disappearing and reappearing in the most unusual of places.

✴ As a child, you always wanted a magic wand and you always believed in fairies.

FAIRY PROTECTION DOOR WREATH SPELL

Before you begin, gather everything you'll need to make a wreath. Choose some flowers – try to find some with silver leaves, or spray some of them with silver glitter, as you want this to shine in the moonlight. You could also dab fluorescent paint on the tips of the leaves, or on some artificial leaves, to make them glow in the moonlight. Use plenty of flowers, as the fairies love flowers. In fact, they love all things from nature, so you could also add pine cones, acorns and even berries. You may wish to choose a flower that represents something particular, such as love (rose), wealth (orchid) or protection (hyacinth). You will also need the wreath frame, which you can pick up quite easily at a craft store or online along with ribbon and some bells.

As you make your wreath, say these words:

> **Round and round the moon goes.**
> **Bless all who pass through these doors.**
> **Let no negativity enter, no sorrows.**
> **Fairy Moon on this blessed night,**
> **Grace us forever, blessed from your light.**

As you weave your wreath, make sure to add the bells for the Queen of the Fairies, who is said to ride out on a snow-white horse looking for mortals to lure away to Fairyland for seven years. (The bells are a supernatural door knock to the other world and the land of Fae.)

TRADITIONAL
WITCHES

This world of witches encompasses the traditional and familiar types of witches, such as the Hereditary Witch or the Eclectic Witch. These witch types are linked to the forms of witchcraft that have been written about in books and shown in various films. They also feature the religious quality of witchcraft, for example the Wiccan Witch, a follower of Wicca. The witch types in this chapter are the established ones that found popularity in the 1960s and 1970s, and we owe a great deal to them, as they paved the way for the newer types of witch we see today. Welcome to the world of the Witch.

What appeals to you most?

a. broomstick
b. cauldron
c. athame
d. candle
e. pentagram/pentacle

What is your favourite part of the house?

a. garden
b. kitchen
c. bathroom
d. bedroom
e. living room

Which of these genres do you prefer?

a. fantasy
b. sci-fi
c. action
d. horror
e. romance

Which of these famous witches do you identify with?

a. Hermione Granger (*Harry Potter*)
b. Prue Halliwell (*Charmed*)
c. Sabrina Spellman (*Sabrina the Teenage Witch/The Chilling Adventures of Sabrina*)
d. Sally Owens (*Practical Magic*)
e. Sarah Bailey (*The Craft*)

Which core aesthetic are you attracted to?

a. fairycore
b. cottagecore
c. witchcore
d. forestcore
e. Grandmacore

Your friends are organising a fancy-dress party. You intend to go as:

a. a fairy
b. a witch
c. a clown
d. a vampire
e. a Greek/Roman goddess

Your friends would describe you as:

a. dreamy, vague
b. traditional and dependable
c. scatty but with lots of ideas
d. intuitive, psychic
e. dogmatic and disciplined

When it comes to rules, you think:

a. what are rules?
b. I will follow them, but I don't want to
c. rules need to be broken
d. I'll do what's right, thanks
e. I love rules

The time from history you most identify with is:

a. none, but I would love to live
   in Camelot with Merlin
b. ancient Greece/Rome/Egypt
c. the time of Anglo-Saxons and Vikings
d. Tudor times
e. 1940-1950s

MOSTLY AS: HEDGEWITCH

The Hedgewitch is the witch that nothing and no one can pin down.
They are a law unto themselves, and they practise solitarily. They
have no need for anyone else and prefer to live in their other world,
as these witches travel the borders or the hedges of old. They have
powerful spells of transformation and travel, and will eagerly
seek out the other realms of existence. They are at their happiest
amongst the trees and forests, and are not afraid of the dark.

MOSTLY BS: HEREDITARY WITCH

The Hereditary Witch is a practitioner of the Craft who comes
from a long line of witches. Their mothers or fathers could have
passed down the magical practices to them, or perhaps it skipped
a generation and they learned it from their grandparents. Either
way, the Hereditary Witch is a witch with magic in their veins
and knowledge in their hearts.

MOSTLY CS: ECLECTIC WITCH

An Eclectic Witch is a witch who will practise two or more ways.
Their magical practice may change with the seasons, from being a
Kitchen Witch (page 119) in the winter months to a more outbound
one, such as a White Witch (page 35), in the summer.

MOSTLY DS: INTUITIVE WITCH

An Intuitive Witch is not to be confused with a Divination Witch
(page 107), as this witch is someone who relies on instinct, which
is usually spontaneous and not planned. They are highly clairvoyant
and clairsentient, and can detect feelings immediately when
walking into a room, before or after an argument.

MOSTLY ES: WICCAN WITCH

The Wiccan Witch is a witch who follows the religion of Wicca
as first devised by either Gerald Gardner or Alex Sanders, whose
form of Wicca was called Alexandrian Wicca, while the former
was Gardnerian Wicca. Wicca is now recognised as a religion and
comes under the umbrella of Paganism. The Wiccan Witch will
follow the Pagan Wheel of the Year and may be part of a coven.
The Wiccan Witch will follow the Wiccan Rede: an' it harm none,
do what ye wilt.

THE HEDGEWITCH

CHARACTER
Free, untameable, pure, innocent

LUCKY COLOUR
Pink

LUCKY ANIMAL
Rabbit

MAGICAL PRACTICE
Nature spells, charms and brews,
travelling spells

DESCRIPTION

The Hedgewitch is a bit of an oddball, to say the least, as no two are ever the same. One of the reasons for this is that the Hedgewitch is determined by their environment, so if a Hedgewitch lives in the city, their magical practices will be different to those of a country Hedgewitch or a coastal Hedgewitch. This is due to not only the plants and trees that grow in each area, but also the energies or elemental beings found in these areas. The Hedgewitch is a mystical and esoteric witch. They will regularly seek out the elemental worlds like the Fae Witch (page 86), but are not just confined to the world of Fae, venturing into other realms also. Traditionally the Hedgewitch was defined as a solitary practitioner of the Craft and was always a woman, but times change, and although they will still be solitary in their magical practice, they can be any gender.

STRENGTHS

The Hedgewitch's strength is in their solitary existence, as they are incredibly independent and have no need for any social contact. These witches know that although they are alone, they are never truly on their own. This independence makes them incredibly self-sufficient, which is a powerful attribute and ensures they can turn absolutely anything and everything into a magical resource.

SIGNS YOU COULD BE A HEDGEWITCH

✳ You love being on your own as you know that you are not alone.

✳ You often go off the beaten track and will find yourself in weird and wonderful places. You may try to return to them, but can never find them again.

✳ You are not afraid of the dark and relish the mysterious and unexplained questions in life.

✳ You follow your instinct even when others think it is wrong.

MEDITATION TRAVELLING SPELL

One of the many magical things about a Hedgewitch is their ability to 'travel'; they can spiritually drift away, even when you're talking to them! Very much individual and solitary, the Hedgewitch's magical practice is unique; so much so that no two are ever the same.

A Hedgewitch's 'travels' are a form of meditation and can be performed anywhere and everywhere. A Hedgewitch will usually like to go travelling via different weather or seasonal phenomena, such as autumn mists, summer rain showers, winter frosts and spring gales.

Try this Hedgewitch's Meditation Travelling Spell. On a windy, misty or frosty day, go for a walk on your own in nature, leaving all distractions behind. As you walk, notice your breathing, taking deep, steady breaths. Become aware of your surroundings, such as the wind in the trees, the birds singing and the sounds and sensations of walking alone through nature. When you are ready and feeling very calm, open your arms out wide on either side and say, as you continue to walk:

> **Here I am, here and now,**
> **But I can fly, when dreams allow,**
> **On air, water, earth and fire of storms.**
> **Let go and release as my soul stretches**
> **and yawns. Go now, and be free.**
> **Travelling forever, blessed be.**

Close your eyes and let go of all worries and thoughts, then become aware of your surroundings again. You may notice that everything has become still, with no wind or birds singing, and complete silence around you. Relish this moment as time seems to stand still, for it will not last long. When everything starts again, you will feel refreshed.

THE HEREDITARY WITCH

CHARACTER
Traditional, aloof, biased, powerful

LUCKY COLOUR
Cyan

LUCKY ANIMAL
Cat

MAGICAL PRACTICE
Highly knowledgeable in all traditional
areas of magic, from spells to charms

DESCRIPTION

A Hereditary Witch is exactly what their name suggests: someone who comes from a parent who is a witch and/or a long line of witches. When it comes to hereditary witchcraft, it may skip a generation or two, or even more. Hereditary witchcraft boils down to the question of what witchcraft really is, anyway: a religion, a folklore, a tradition, an oral custom? Therefore, ask parents, grandparents, or even great-grandparents if you are lucky enough to have them, and enquire if there are any specific recipes, saying or customs in your family. Do they have little rituals or remedies? For example, perhaps if you are stung by nettles, your grandma advises you to rub the sting with a dock leaf. Or maybe you have an upset stomach and your auntie tells you to drink some mint tea. These are all indicators of the possibility of folklore or witchcraft, somewhere along the line.

STRENGTHS

Hereditary witches are particularly powerful users of ancestral magic. In other words, they may call upon the ancestors or ask for their help in a variety of ways, including rituals, séances, the lighting of candles, keeping photos of their loved ones around or using a particular item that once belonged to their ancestor in their magic.

SIGNS YOU COULD BE A HEREDITARY WITCH

✳ You love history, especially family history, and may have even begun investigating your family tree.

✳ Family members remark that you remind them of an ancestor.

✳ Your family have artefacts that are passed down from generation to generation, which you value very much.

✳ You have the same birthmark as several members of your family in several generations.

✳ You family have strange superstitions and traditions.

SPELL TO CONNECT WITH AN ANCESTOR

If you want to connect with an ancestor, try this spell. Sit at a table with two chairs at either end – one for you and one for your ancestor. In the middle of the table, light a blue candle, and place a pen and paper in front of you, as well as a photo of your ancestor and/or something that once belonged to them. You may have never met this relative, as they could have passed on a long time before you were born. If you know their name, say it in the spell; otherwise, just use the word 'ancestor'. Into the blue candle, say these words:

**I call upon (name, if known), ancestor of mine.
I ask you to come now in this space and time.
Your wisdom and power I do seek.
As your descendant, I would like to meet.**

Wait for a couple of moments. The candle may flicker, or you may smell a distinctive smell such as flowers or even tobacco smoke. These are all signs that your ancestor is present. If you have questions, ask them, speaking slowly. You may hear the responses, or you may have flashes of the answers in your mind. Whatever you experience, write it down. When you are finished, politely thank them for their responses and for coming to meet you, but kindly ask them to return to their realm. Blow out the candle. The more times you do this, the easier it will become.

THE ECLECTIC WITCH

CHARACTER
Independent, freedom-loving,
creative, quick-thinking

LUCKY COLOUR
Cream

LUCKY ANIMAL
Goose

MAGICAL PRACTICE
Highly knowledgeable when it comes to
correspondences, and will seek to weave
magic in all its wondrous colours with
spells, incantations, charms and brews

DESCRIPTION

The Eclectic Witch is a witch who picks from all the other different witch types and chooses how and what they want to practice and when. Many Eclectic Witches choose different types of witchcraft in conjunction with the changing of seasons. For example, during the summer months, an Eclectic Witch may borrow elements of a Fae Witch (page 87), while in the winter months, they may choose to follow certain ways of the Lunar Witch (page 71) or the Green Witch (page 31). It all depends on the Eclectic Witch in question. Like the Hedgewitch (page 95), no two are ever really the same.

STRENGTHS

Although an Eclectic Witch may appear to be a Jack of all trades and master of none, it is wise to remember the full quote when referring to these witches: 'Jack of all trades is a master of none, but oftentimes better than a master of one.' In other words, at certain times, it is wise to know about many things, rather than knowing a lot about one specific thing. In the same way, the Eclectic Witch is incredibly knowledgeable in all aspects of magic, and can apply themselves with diligence to any that take their fancy, which is a remarkable strength to have.

SIGNS YOU COULD BE AN ECLECTIC WITCH

✳ You get bored with things quite easily.

✳ You love to look at lots of different programmes on TV and are always flitting to and fro with the remote.

✳ You constantly change your phone.

✳ You change your fashion sense, style and hair colour often.

✳ You tend not to care what others think of you and are content with your own choices.

FULL MOON RELAXATION SPELL

An Eclectic Witch's mind is always racing, but in order to perform magic they need to learn to relax. Relaxation is very important for our mental wellbeing and state of mind. Although the full moon can make it hard to sleep, you can utilise this phase to help you unwind.

Try this technique on the night of a full moon, preferably at the weekend. Turn off all phones and electrical equipment, such as your TV, computer and lights. This is important, as so many people naturally leave the lights on throughout the house, even in rooms they are not using. Turn off all the lights that you safely can, and take a bath or shower by candlelight. Afterwards, making sure you will not be interrupted, lie flat on your bed, with your arms by your sides, palms facing down. Concentrate on your breathing: in through your nose and out through your mouth. Now say:

My mind is racing but I cannot think.
My thoughts are buzzing and will not shrink.
I stress and worry but cannot know.
Too many worries won't let me go.
I am not thinking clearly because I think too much.
I cannot see what is in front of me as such.
Help my mind to rest and chill.
Relaxation is an ideal pill.

Imagine a blue light flowing down from the moon, completely encasing you in blue healing light. Your mind sees only blue with no thoughts or worries: just a blue colour completely flowing around it. Relax for as long as you want and as deeply as you want, but before you drift off to sleep, make sure you have safely extinguished all candles.

THE INTUITIVE WITCH

CHARACTER
Instinctive, psychic, changeable, trusting

LUCKY COLOUR
Purple

LUCKY ANIMAL
Duck

MAGICAL PRACTICE
Energy placement magic

DESCRIPTION

The Intuitive Witch is incredibly instinctive, and is someone who can walk into a room and know immediately if there has been an argument. Be careful if you're talking about an Intuitive Witch behind their back, because they will know what was said and by whom. These witches are great with animals and children, and can instinctively tune in to both to see what ails them if they are under the weather. As such, Intuitive Witches can make great teachers and vets. These are the witches from whom you cannot hide a secret; therefore, you can forget about throwing a surprise birthday party for an Intuitive Witch, as they will know immediately what you are up to.

STRENGTHS

An Intuitive Witch is especially powerful when they use blessing spells. Due to their instinctive power to know what others need, they can cast a very strong blessing spell on anyone and on any object. Blessing spells can be used on anything and for any purpose; you can bless your car, your home, your garden or your pet, or even important possessions that need to be kept safe.

SIGNS YOU COULD BE AN INTUITIVE WITCH

✴ You know if someone is keeping a secret from you.

✴ You can sense if someone is ill.

✴ You are very clairsentient, which literally means 'all feeling' (while clairvoyant means 'all seeing').

✴ You tend to follow your own instincts, even when others think you are wrong.

✴ You always seem to be right about things, including people, pets and events.

✴ You are a great judge of character.

WITCH'S LADDER DREAMWORK CHARMSPELL

The Witch's Ladder can be used for all manner of spells, incantations and ritualism, but one of its uses is to catch dreams to work with.

To make a Witch's Ladder, you need no fewer than five feathers and no more than ten. Go for a walk out in nature and see if you can find any feathers. They can be from crows, pheasants, pigeons, hawks – any type of feather you can find. You can use craft feathers if you wish. You need two long feathers of the same length to form the sides, and then about three shorter ones to create the steps. You'll also need black ribbon.

On the night of the dark moon (a night when the moon is not visible), make your ladder by placing a long feather vertically and attaching one of the short feathers near the bottom of the long feather, so that the short feather is positioned as the bottom step. Secure it by wrapping the black ribbon around the two in a figure-of-eight motion, then twist the ribbon around as you go up to the next feather step. Repeat until you have at least three steps. Carry the ribbon over to the other long feather and repeat the process coming down the other side. As you wrap and weave, say this incantation:

Weave the feathers of flight.
Catching dreams from the night.
Dark moon rising, shield this from the light.

Repeat this until you have made your Witch's Ladder and hang it above your bed. In the morning, carefully clasp the ladder in both hands, close your eyes, and remember the dreams you had in order to work with them. You will receive flashes of inspiration or images of strange things; write these down immediately. Dreamwork is a long process of understanding the signs and symbols, and you will learn that on dark moon nights, strange dreams appear even more for some reason.

THE WICCAN WITCH

CHARACTER
Traditional, dependable,
team-player, work-focused

LUCKY COLOUR
Black

LUCKY ANIMAL
Crow

MAGICAL PRACTICE
All aspects of traditional magic

DESCRIPTION

A Wiccan Witch is someone who practices Wicca, a form of witchcraft that was derived in the 1950s by British civil servant Gerald Gardner. Wicca is an Anglo-Saxon word that literally means 'craft of the wise'. It is a coven-based form of witchcraft. A coven is a closed group of people with an exclusive membership, and usually you can only join through an invitation from the High Priestess or High Priest who governs them. The coven will generally meet at least once a month for a full moon ritual, which is called an Esbat and involves calling down the four quarters, which are North, East, South and West and also the elements they represent and casting a circle. Wiccans follow the Wheel of the Year instead of or alongside the general calendar year of festivals, but their holidays are different. The Wiccan Wheel of the Year begins not in January but on Halloween, otherwise known as Samhain.

STRENGTHS

The strength of the Wiccan Witch lies in their ritual magic, which is generally conducted as a group. These witches are connected to each other via their beliefs, and as they come together to practice, their power doubles, trebles and so on. Their rituals and festival magic are potent forms of magic.

SIGNS YOU COULD BE A WICCAN WITCH

✴ You like to be part of a group or team.

✴ You don't like doing things on your own.

✴ You like to perform rituals.

✴ You prefer to follow rules and guidelines.

✴ You feel a strong affinity to Halloween, and feel such a connection to it that it has always felt the end of the year for you, with a sense that things begin again afterwards.

SAMHAIN MOON POTENT POTION

This is a magical potion to brew up to protect a house, a car, a person or a pet. It requires either the waxing or closest full moon of Samhain.

INGREDIENTS

250 ml (8 fl oz/1 cup) water, 3 tablespoons poppy milk, 3 tablespoons ground cinnamon, 1 sage leaf, crushed, 3 drops of milk thistle

METHOD

Combine all the ingredients in a little saucepan – or a cauldron, if you have one – and gradually bring to the boil. Stir deasil (clockwise) and as you do so, say these words:

> **I call upon Samhain moon power**
> **To bless this potion in every hour.**
> **Protect those with whom this brew doth meet.**
> **With milk of the poppy and highlanders' tears,**
> **This spell is now complete.**
> **Let my loved ones be protected for years.**

When the mixture has boiled, carefully remove it from the heat and allow to cool in light of the Samhain moon. In the morning, bottle and label it, and use within the year.

To use, sprinkle three drops of it on your car, or on your pet's collar, or sprinkle it around the house. For the protection of a person or yourself, put three drops into a glass of water, stir then drink.

CREATIVE WITCHES

The witch types in this chapter are some of the most creative witches around. These witches might be artists and designers in their working lives, and the magic they bring to their creations is extremely powerful. They are very practical in that they can create anything, and once they put their mind to it, their creations can manifest into wonderful pieces of art, design or even food. This chapter is where the Kitchen Witch and the Book Witch reside. The witches found in this group are aware of their own unique imaginative powers and can express themselves accordingly. Welcome to the world of creative witches.

Your ideal house would have:

a. an amazing kitchen
b. an art studio
c. a library
d. a secret magic room
e. a craft room with anything and everything

**You have offered to host a dinner party.
Your friends respond by:**

a. jumping for joy as your food is superb
b. accepting, but seeming intrigued by what
culinary experiment you will serve
c. nodding politely, but suggesting they
bring a pizza
d. recoiling in horror
e. saying, 'No, let's go to a restaurant instead'

**You have planned a day out at the shopping
mall. You immediately aim for the:**

a. kitchen accessories and utensils store
b. bookstore, especially the art and craft section
c. speciality/curiosity/witchy shop
d. coffee shop, so you can people-watch all day
e. the haberdashery department, from which
you will never emerge again

Which mythical creature would you like to be?

a. a brownie
b. a muse
c. a unicorn
d. a dragon
e. an elf

Which *Alice in Wonderland* character would you be?

a. the Mad Hatter
b. the Red Queen
c. the Caterpillar
d. the Cheshire Cat
e. Alice

Who would you bring back to life from the past?

a. Julia Child
b. Claude Monet
c. Jean-Jacques Rousseau
d. Albert Einstein
e. Coco Chanel

You see a ghost. What do you do?

a. invite them to join you for tea
b. grab your phone/camera to take a photo
c. make a note of the encounter in your diary
d. talk to them for hours
e. RUN

If you could live in a novel, what would it be?

a. *Eat, Pray, Love*
b. *A Portrait of the Artist as a Young Man*
c. *Pride and Prejudice*
d. *James and the Giant Peach*
e. *How to Make an American Quilt*

116

MOSTLY AS: KITCHEN WITCH

The Kitchen Witch is a practitioner of the Craft who hones her magical practice in the kitchen. This witch not only makes magical potions, lotions and concoctions, but the food she serves will also have the added benefit of magic. Every meal a Kitchen Witch cooks will have a spell attached to it, to help, heal and guide the recipient with every morsel.

MOSTLY BS: ART WITCH

The Art Witch is a practitioner of the Craft who is incredibly creative and artistic. The Art Witch will practise magic through all the artistic forms: anything from music and poetry, to dance, pottery, painting, drawing or any other art or craft form to which they feel drawn. As witches, they speak through art and their magical work is some of the most beautiful around.

MOSTLY CS: BOOK WITCH

The Book Witch is a seeker of esoteric and occult knowledge who will keep a meticulous record of their own magical practices, and will have a large selection of various types of grimoires as well as their own Book of Shadows.

MOSTLY DS: THE HEXAFOIL WITCH

The Hexafoil Witch or the symbolic witch finds their magic and strength in symbols and signs, including the medieval witch symbols which are cast upon buildings such as churches and portable objects such as chests and heavy stone fonts. They practise sigil magic and the witch's alphabet, also known as the Theban Script, is a primary source of power for them. In palm-reading, these witches will often be found to have an X on their palm.

MOSTLY ES: PRACTICAL WITCH

The Practical Witch is a witch who connects with many different forms of magic but is always drawn to the practical, hence the name. They will always have a spell on standby and their bags will be filled with crystals and herbs. In many ways, their motto is, 'Be prepared.' They are the type of witch you can always rely on for a magical way out of things.

THE KITCHEN WITCH

CHARACTER
Practical, methodical,
organised, scientific

LUCKY COLOUR
Teal

LUCKY ANIMAL
Sheep

MAGICAL PRACTICE
Potions and brews

DESCRIPTION

One of the main misconceptions about a Kitchen Witch is that they work only in a kitchen. However, the Kitchen Witch can also be known as the Hearth Witch or the Home Witch. Traditionally, the hearth was the main source of heat in the home, such as the fire or the stove, which was never really allowed to go out. It was the heart of the home, a place where the family members gathered. As a result, Kitchen Witches are often regarded as the symbolic centre of their family, as they are nurturing and caring. Therefore, kitchen witchery is not only about cooking up delicious meals and potions but also the general welfare and wellbeing of family and friends.

STRENGTHS

A Kitchen Witch's strength is their ability to make something out of nothing. They can literally manifest a three-course meal from hardly any ingredients. Yet this ability to manifest out of thin air is not only limited to the kitchen; in many areas of their lives, when things are amiss, they can literally pull out anything when required. They are always prepared.

SIGNS YOU COULD BE A KITCHEN WITCH

✶ You are a real homebody. And although you like going on holiday, you love coming home.

✶ You love to be surrounded by family and friends.

✶ You love to cook for loved ones, and your food is always delicious.

✶ Although your entire home is lovely and welcoming, people always seem to congregate in the kitchen.

✶ At a party, even in another house, you will find yourself pulled towards the kitchen and will probably remain there for most of the evening.

HOME AT LAST HOT CHOCOLATE SPELL

If your friends and family have been away from home, whether for a long trip or just because they have been at work all day and are in need of a treat, then make a welcoming hot chocolate drink and turn it into a big 'hug in a mug' spell.

This makes one cup, but you can scale up the ingredients to make more.

INGREDIENTS

250 ml (8 fl oz/1 cup) milk or milk alternative (coconut milk works well for hot chocolate), 125 ml (4 fl oz/½ cup) double (heavy) cream or alternative, 1 tablespoon granulated sugar (optional), 250 ml (8 fl oz) grated chocolate, milk or dark, depending on your taste whipped cream, to serve

METHOD

Combine the milk and cream in a small saucepan and heat over a medium heat until small bubbles appear around the edges; do not boil. Remove from the heat and stir in the sugar and grated chocolate, then place over a low heat until all the chocolate has melted, slowly stirring all the time. As you stir, say these words:

Home at last, chocolate goes so fast.
Sweet and warm, as tender as can be.
Come on in and talk to me.
This drink is a big hug,
Lovely and warm, just in a mug.
Leave your worries at the door.
This hot chocolate will leave you wanting more.

Remove from the heat and serve with love and a big dollop of whipped cream on top.

THE ART WITCH

CHARACTER
Imaginative, dreamy,
creative, quirky

LUCKY COLOUR
Magenta

LUCKY ANIMAL
Swallow

MAGICAL PRACTICE
Visual art forms, but will also include
poetry, music and dance

DESCRIPTION

Art Witches live and breathe art in all its many forms, and every part of their practice will revolve around art. Nature itself becomes their art supply depot, and they will create paintings, sculptures and drawings from rocks, stones, twigs, leaves and flowers. Everything within nature is at their disposal and used in their magic.

These witches are adept at colour magic in all its wondrous forms, from candle magic to ribbon magic. The Art Witch will know the correspondences of colours and will weave these into their practice.

STRENGTHS

Art Witches are particularly in tune with the power of different objects, places and spaces. They are incredibly good at visualisation, and can often see paintings come to life. For example, when an Art Witch stands in front of one of Monet's famous *Water Lilies* paintings, they can visualise the water gently moving and the willow trees swaying in a soft breeze. If you stand close to an Art Witch, you can see this phenomenon too, as they have the power to visualise and project that experience through art, time and space.

Art Witches are also good with manifestation techniques, and can create powerful vision boards.

SIGNS YOU COULD BE AN ART WITCH

✳ You love art in all its many forms, and you are at your happiest when drawing, writing, designing, dancing or making music.

✳ Time seems to move at a strange pace with you, depending on what you're doing.

✳ You see colours all the time; they seem to jump out at you wherever you are.

✳ You notice textures and shapes, and can see patterns where others do not.

MAGICAL MANIFESTING MOOD BOARD SPELL

Many creative people begin their art and craft projects by making a mood board. A mood board is a collection or collage of images, text, objects and colours arranged in a particular composition. The creator may pick a theme, which can be anything; for example from a feeling, season, car, sofa, etc. The Art Witch has the power to manifest with their mood boards, which can be made for anything at all. Here is an example of a manifesting mood board spell.

Use a pinboard or hard piece of card, preferably A3 size, so you have plenty of space to fill with your images. Your mood board can be for absolutely anything you desire, but for this purpose, let's imagine it is for a holiday. Pick out images of the holiday you want, cutting them out from magazines or travel brochures, or printing pictures from the internet. Think of the colours you will see; perhaps you will choose varying shades of blue for the swimming pool or ocean. Think of the plants you might see or the food you might eat. Consider the clothes you will wear, adding fabric samples if you have them, and stick them on your board. Arrange them in a way that pleases you. One of the key things about a mood board is that you start with one idea in mind, and then everything else flows from it.

After you have made your mood board, place both hands on the board and say these words:

On this board I will make, **My dreams and desires come to pass. Manifesting holidays** (*or whatever it is you are manifesting*) **that are great**, **With these pictures**, **colours and shapes. Come now into my reality. That which I manifest**, **now come to me.**

Close your eyes and imagine yourself at the beach or by the pool. Imagine the sounds, sights and smells. Perform this spell once a week for a month to manifest your dream – though it might not take that long to manifest, as you could suddenly find yourself receiving a holiday as a surprise gift or competition prize!

THE BOOK WITCH

CHARACTER
Studious, solitary,
friendly, inquisitive

LUCKY COLOUR
Navy Blue

LUCKY ANIMAL
Tortoise

MAGICAL PRACTICE
Ancient magic from old grimoires,
spells of all varieties, but especially
ones that need to be written down,
not just spoken

DESCRIPTION

The Book Witch is one of those rare witches who is wonderful to know and yet very rarely socialises, as they prefer their own company, happily living among their books, diaries and journals. These witches are incredibly knowledgeable. Not only do they enjoy reading books, but many also write them. They will also know about how to care for and repair antique books, and may work in the conservation of ancient manuscripts. These witches will have an array of witchcraft books and grimoires or Books of Shadows.

STRENGTHS

The record-keeping of magical practices is the Book Witch's strength, so their Book of Shadows will be the most powerful of all. A Book of Shadows, otherwise known as a grimoire, is like a journal or diary in which a practitioner of magic will keep a record of their magical workings, such as spells, potions, recipes, correspondence charts, and a whole array of magical and mystical things.

SIGNS YOU COULD BE A BOOK WITCH

* You can take ages to describe something or to relay a story, as you go into so much detail that it becomes a saga like *War and Peace*.

* You are walking encyclopaedia, and friends are always asking you 'What does this mean?'.

* You prefer your own company.

* Your favourite place to shop is a book shop.

* You love stationery, and have an array of pens, pencils and staplers, as well as pencil cases galore.

* You like to keep a diary or journal, writing in it regularly.

BOOK WITCH
KNOWLEDGE SPELL

Knowledge really is power, and when we know the facts about something, we feel empowered. Knowledge comes in many forms. Academics have written about the seven sources of knowledge, and believe it or not, superstition and intuition are two of the main sources. The others are authority, tenacity, rationalism, empiricism and science. Unfortunately, today, we tend to think of knowledge mainly in terms of the latter, with empiricism and science at its heart. Yet superstition and intuition are equally important – if not more important – in the development of our knowledge.

The Blue Moon brings intuitive powers that can increase your knowledge of the world around you, and although it is a rare event, it is an opportunity to take stock and set yourself on a new path. On the night of the Blue Moon, open yourself to the intuitive aspect of this rare celestial event and ask for intuitive knowledge to come to you. Go outside, raise your hands to the moon and say:

> **Faith and belief and superstition galore,**
> **Blue Moon magic, increase my intuition more.**
> **Where I am at here and now –**
> **Is it right or is it wrong?**
> **Give me insight for what is right.**
> **On this blessed Blue Moon night.**

Then, in your journal or Book of Shadows, write down the images or feelings you may experience. You may have flashes of yourself being in a different job, or you may experience a sudden burst of enthusiasm for going back to school to learn something different. These are all inspirations coming to you from the Blue Moon to get you back on track. Remember to record everything you experience – but as a Book Witch, doing so will come naturally to you.

THE HEXAFOIL WITCH

CHARACTER
Intriguing, fascinating,
captivating, methodical

LUCKY COLOUR
Orange

LUCKY ANIMAL
Dog

MAGICAL PRACTICE
Symbolic magic, sigil magic,
codes, secrets

DESCRIPTION

The Hexafoil Witch will see signs, symbols and patterns in everything, and all will hold a meaning. This is the witch of secret languages and strange codes, as the name suggests. The hexafoil or daisy wheel is a symbol that looks like six petals within a circle. It is found across England and Wales, usually on church doors or walls. The hexafoil was believed to trap and confuse evil spirits. The specific witch type of the Hexafoil Witch has developed over recent years, and is someone who draws their magic in wonderful designs. A Hexafoil Witch does not necessarily have to be particularly artistic to create their sigil designs, as nowadays there are plenty of great sigil apps to use.

STRENGTHS

Hexafoil Witches are ideal sigilists. A sigil is a specially designed symbol that has magical power. Many Hexafoil Witches design sigils for their spells and rituals, and will carve their specific design into a candle which is then lit. As the candle burns down, the sigil is activated and the spell is cast.

SIGNS YOU COULD BE A HEXAFOIL WITCH

✴ You like puzzles and jigsaws.

✴ You love Sudoku.

✴ As a child, you were always practising your signature, and would add flourishes to your name, like putting a love hearts over an 'i'.

✴ You are intrigued and captivated by ancient Egyptian hieroglyphs and strange ancient writing - you have probably even tried writing your name in hieroglyphs.

✴ As a child, you sometimes spoke in a strange code with your friends.

SIGIL AWAKE SPELL

A sigil is a major part of the Hexafoil Witch's arsenal, and although they can look incredibly complicated, they are actually very easy to make. First, you need your intention. Let's say you have a test or exam coming up that you need to pass. You might write:

I want to pass this test

Now, take out all the vowels, so disregard a, e, i, o, u. Therefore, it becomes:

Wnt t pss ths tst

Next, delete all the repeated letters, so you are left with:

Wnt ps h

Now, this is where the fun begins as you design your sigil. You can turn the letters upside down, on their sides, or rotate them in a circle to make them all connect; the possibilities are endless. You can create your design in any way you desire. If you get stuck, there are dozens of sigil apps which might inspire you.

After you have settled on your design, draw your sigil on a fresh piece of paper and put your right hand over it as you say:

I invoke this spell for me.
This sigil now awakes, so mote it be.

Your sigil spell is now live and active. After the sigil has done its work and is no longer needed, you can disperse it by burying it in the garden or safely burning it by tossing it on to the fire - and remember to say thank you to it.

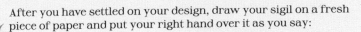

THE PRACTICAL WITCH

CHARACTER
Resourceful, entrepreneurial,
creative, frugal

LUCKY COLOUR
Burgundy

LUCKY ANIMAL
Fox

MAGICAL PRACTICE
Charms, potions, magical crafts

MAGICAL SPECIALITY
Charms that are handmade
from start to finish

DESCRIPTION

The Practical Witch is extremely creative, although perhaps not in the traditional artistic sense. They may not produce paintings and portraits; their magic lies in the wonderful things they create through sewing, pottery, knitting and even flower arranging. These witches can make great interior designers and know instinctively which colour schemes, materials and fabrics are needed to create the right ambience in any room, along with space, light and magic. The Practical Witch is also known as the Craft Witch, the Sewing Witch or the Design Witch. These witches enhance the objects they craft with magical intent, so never refuse anything offered to you by a Practical Witch: they create very powerful objects that can help and heal, and enable you to manifest your greatest desires.

STRENGTHS

The Practical Witch's strength is their ability to infuse anything they are working on with such power that it becomes a charmed item. That is why a Practical Witch will never make anything to give to someone if they are upset or angry, as the magic they manifest may turn into a curse and bring the recipient nothing but bad luck.

SIGNS YOU COULD BE A PRACTICAL WITCH

✴ As a child, you were always making things.

✴ You excelled at design, woodwork and/or sewing at school.

✴ You are always keeping things, such as empty boxes, glass jars and wrapping paper, to use as materials later.

✴ You love upcycling used items, redesigning them into something fantastic and new.

✴ You always keep torn clothes, as the material can be reused to create no end of things, from quilts, bags and cushions to new clothing items, like turning a dress into a skirt.

ORDER-ORDER SPELL

One thing that the Practical Witch excels at is organisation. These witches love nothing better than to have order in their lives, from having the tidiest cupboards to a colour-coordinated wardrobe. Decluttering is a favourite pastime of the Practical Witch.

If you want to begin to live the life of a Practical Witch, start decluttering or putting things in order, whether that's in your wardrobe, your kitchen or wherever you feel a little order is needed. If you're starting in the kitchen, begin with one cupboard and completely empty it. Check the use-by dates on food and spices, and throw out any that are out of date. Check your crockery for cracked and chipped plates and cups, and either find a good use for them in your projects or give to a like-minded witch friend such as an Art witch or Green Witch for use in the garden.

When you have sorted the contents of the cupboard, clean the empty cupboard with a natural disinfectant. Try making your own by mixing two parts water, with one part white vinegar. Add 10 drops of essential lemon oil and pour the mixture into a spray bottle. As you spritz the cupboard, say these words:

> **Order in my life.**
> **Chaos is strife.**
> **Order that I seek,**
> **Clear and neat.**
> **Everything has purpose,**
> **And everything has its place.**
> **Bring order to this space.**

When you're finished, allow the cupboard to dry, then put the contents back and begin the process again with another cupboard.

Last Words

Sadly, we have reached the end of our journey down the path of witch types. I hope you have enjoyed this book and are now a little clearer on the ways of the witch.

Although we have come to the end of this book, it is the beginning of a way of life. You will have learned that the scope of witchcraft is huge, and although we have looked at twenty-five different types of witch, there is so much more to learn. We have only touched upon the tiniest corner. Witchcraft encompasses every aspect and every corner of life, from candles and food, to the zodiac, plants and animals, crystals, traditions, spirits and elementals – and more. It is a lifestyle, and you have just begun your journey.

I suggest that you now delve a little deeper into your specific witch type for at least a year. Live the seasons of life and follow the Turning of the Wheel, which refers to the transitional year from autumn to winter to spring and summer, a constant turning of the seasonal wheel, complete with our festivals. Before you think about committing to becoming a practitioner of witchcraft. There is an old saying: once a witch, always a witch. If witchcraft is calling you now, you were a probably a witch in a past life.

Embrace the magic, for there is nothing to fear. You have now skimmed the surface of a very old belief system, and there is so much more to learn and experience. Do so with love in your heart and remember, magic always stems from you. It is within you, and it is entirely up to you how you practise.

Blessed be,
Tudorbeth

A Witch's Dictionary

Here are some words and terms that you may be unfamiliar with that many witches use in their everyday practice.

Amulet

An amulet is an object, often a piece of jewellery, that holds special power either to ward off evil or to bring good luck (for example, the evil eye).

Besom

Another name for the wonderful, magical broomstick.

Catoptromancy

Another term for scrying (see below).

Correspondences

Correspondences refer to the connection of everything within the universe, from planets to foods to colours, and even feelings - all are connected to each other.

Deasil

Clockwise.

Elf Shot

A sudden decline in health, often regarded to be the work of witches or fairies.

Familiar

A familiar is an animal or insect that seems to follow the witch wherever they go. The familiar is a lucky protector and guide for the witch.

Hagstone

A naturally occurring stone that has a hole in the middle of it, a hagstone is often thought to bring good luck.

Jinx

A term for feeling hexed or cursed, usually when you are experiencing a run of bad luck.

Kindred spirits

Two or more people with the same interests and attitudes who share a common goal.

Otherkin

Those who believe they are non-human or have an aspect of a non-human entity as a part of them, such as a fairy, vampire, werewolf or nymph.

Poppet

An image of someone or a doll that is used in spells. Poppets are usually used for healing, though they can also used to put curses on someone, often by sticking them with pins.

Scrying

A method of seeing the past, present or future using a reflective surface such as a mirror or a bowl of water. You can also scry with flames, so

you may see things in a candle flame.

Sigil

A symbol or design that has a magical intent and is itself a visual spell.

Transvection

The ability of witches to fly on broomsticks.

Veil

A spiritual barrier that becomes thinner during certain times of the year, such as at Halloween or the spring equinox.

The Wiccan Rede

The main teaching of Wicca. It has become very popular in witch circles nowadays: 'An it harm none, do what ye wilt.'

Widdershins

Anticlockwise.

About the Author

Tudorbeth is a hereditary practitioner of witchcraft and has written many courses on all forms of witchcraft from Hedgewitchery to Ancient Magic. She is the author of numerous books, including *The Hedgewitch's Little Book of Crystal Spells* and *The Hedgewitch's Little Book of Spells, Charms & Brews* (both Llewellyn) and *A Spellbook for the Seasons* (Eddison Books, 2019).

Acknowledgements

Thank you to Kate Burkett, Commissioning Editor of Hardie Grant UK, for seeing the potential of my query. And to Eila Purvis, Senior Editor, who with passion, patience and vision has helped to create a truly wonderful book. You both have magic running through your hearts. Thank you.

Thank you also to Beth and Lucie, without whom the witches and book would not be as enchanted.

Index

Spells and Magical Practices
are in *italics*

Published in 2024 by Hardie Grant Books,

Hardie Grant Books (London)
5th & 6th Floors
52-54 Southwark Street
London SE1 1UN

British Library Cataloguing-in-Publication Data. A catalogue record
for this book is available from the British Library.

The Witch Within
ISBN: 978-1-78488-761-2

10 9 8 7 6 5 4 3 2 1

Publishing Director: Kajal Mistry
Acting Publishing Director: Judith Hannam
Commissioning Editor: Kate Burkett
Senior Editor: Eila Purvis
Design and Art Direction: Beth Free, Studio Nic&Lou
Copy-editor: Tara O'Sullivan
Proofreader: Lucy Rose York
Illustrator: Lucie Louxor (Lucie Corbasson-Guévenoux)
Indexer: Cathy Heath
Production Controller: Martina Georgieva

Sprat font designed by Ethan Nakache
Colour reproduction by p2d
Printed and bound in China by RR Donnelley Asia Printing
Solution Limited